# creepy creatures

Published by Creative Education
P.O. Box 227, Mankato, Minnesota 56002
Creative Education is an imprint of
The Creative Company
www.thecreativecompany.us

Design and production by Ellen Huber
Art direction by Rita Marshall
Printed in the United States of America

Photographs by 123rf (Adrian Hillman), Bigstock
(kovalvs), Dreamstime (Alexstar, Michael Dykstra,
Xunbin Pan, Skydie, Socrates), iStockphoto
(arlindo71, Evgeniy Ayupov, Judith Flacke, Eric
Isselée, marcus jones, Miroslaw Kijewski, Daleen
Loest, Morley Read, TommyIX, vaeenma, Vector
Life), National Geographic Stock (Piotr Naskrecki/
Minden Pictures, Martin Withers/FLPA/Minden
Pictures), Science Photo Library (Dr. Morely
Read), Shutterstock (2happy, Ryan M. Bolton,
Sourav and Joyeeta Chowdhury, gosphotodesign,
Pawel Kielpinski, kurt_G, Dmitrijs Mihejevs), Veer
(jgroupstudios), Wikipedia (Toby Hudson)

Library of Congress Cataloging-in-Publication Data
Bodden, Valerie.
Cockroaches / by Valerie Bodden.
p. cm. — (Creepy creatures)
Summary: A basic introduction to cockroaches,
examining where they live, how they grow, what
they eat, and the unique traits that help to define
them, such as their ability to hold their breath.
Includes bibliographical references and index.
ISBN 978-1-60818-232-9
1. Cockroaches—Juvenile literature. I. Title.
QL505.5.B63 2013
595.7'28—dc23        2011050277

CPSIA: 040913 PO1675
9 8 7 6 5 4 3 2

# CONTENTS

# cockroaches

VALERIE BODDEN

CREATIVE EDUCATION

It is the middle of the night. You need a drink of water. You go to the kitchen and turn on the light. Suddenly, you step on something crunchy. You bend down to take a look.

It is a cockroach!

A cockroach's head points downward instead of straight out from its body

Cockroaches are insects. They have a hard, flattened body with three parts. They have six legs and two **antennae** (*an-TEH-nee*). Many cockroaches have two pairs of wings, too. But they do not usually fly.

Many cockroaches use their wings to get other roaches' attention

Most cockroaches are black or brown. The smallest cockroaches are about the size of an apple seed.

A cockroach uses its antennae to feel and smell things

But the biggest cockroaches
are almost as big as a
six-year-old's hand!

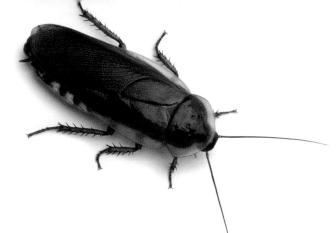

There are about 4,000 kinds of
cockroaches. German cockroaches
live near people around the world.
The rhinoceros cockroach of Australia
is one of the biggest cockroaches.

The rhinoceros cockroach (left)
is also called the giant burrowing cockroach

Mitchell's diurnal cockroach lives in western and southern Australia

Cockroaches can be found almost everywhere in the world. They like warm, **damp** places. Some cockroaches live in forests or caves. Many live in people's houses, too. Cockroaches have to watch out for **predators**. Birds, frogs, lizards, mice, spiders, and centipedes all eat cockroaches.

Cockroaches are food for spiders (left) and lizards (above)

Female cockroaches lay eggs in a special holder called an egg case. Baby cockroaches are called nymphs (*NIMFS*). They look like small adult cockroaches. But they do not have wings. As the nymphs grow, they get too big for their skin. They **molt** so they can keep growing. The last time they molt, they become an adult with wings. Some cockroaches live a few months. Others live more than two years.

This egg case is attached outside the female's abdomen (belly)

Some female roaches carry the egg case inside their bodies until the eggs hatch

Cockroaches eat almost anything. They like people's food and garbage. They eat rotten plants and dead animals, too. They will even eat books and glue!

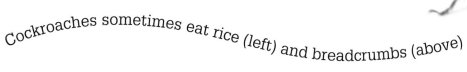

Cockroaches sometimes eat rice (left) and breadcrumbs (above)

Cockroaches can hold their breath for a long time. Sometimes they swim up drainpipes into people's sinks and bathtubs. Cockroaches come out in the dark. They do not like light.

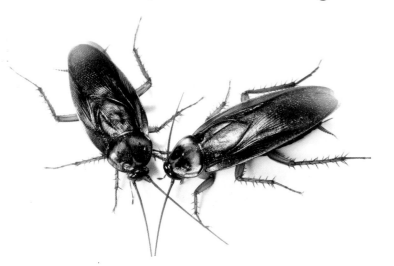

Cockroaches can fit into small spaces such as cracks in walls

The giant cockroach is sometimes sold as a pet

The Madagascar hissing cockroach does not have wings

Some people keep big cockroaches as pets. Other people tell stories or sing songs about cockroaches. It can be fun finding and watching these dark-loving creepy creatures!

## MAKE A COCKROACH

Make a cockroach by cutting an oval (egg) shape out of a black piece of construction paper. Cut a pipe cleaner in half, and glue the two pieces to the top of the oval for antennae. Take two more pipe cleaners, and cut each into three pieces. These will be the legs. Glue three legs to each side of the oval. Then glue your cockroach to the top of a craft stick to make your own cockroach puppet!

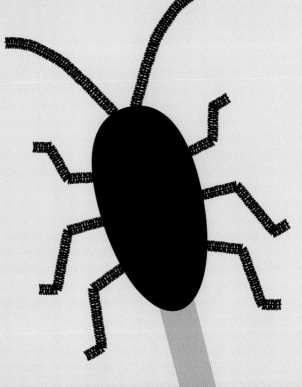

# GLOSSARY

**antennae:** feelers on the heads of some insects that are used to touch, smell, and taste things

**damp:** a little bit wet

**molt:** to lose a shell or layer of skin and grow a new, larger one

**predators:** animals that kill and eat other animals

## READ MORE

Green, Emily K. *Cockroaches*. Minneapolis: Bellwether Media, 2007.

Helget, Nicole. *Cockroaches*. Mankato, Minn.: Creative Education, 2008.

## WEB SITES

Pestworld for Kids

http://www.pestworldforkids.org/cockroaches.html

Learn about different types of cockroaches that have become pests to people.

Roach World

http://kids.discovery.com/tell-me/animals/bug-world/roach-world

Learn about a cockroach's body and its life.

## INDEX